M000034562

ADVOCACY WORDS
A Thesaurus

William Drennan

GP|Solo

ABA General Practice, Solo & Small Firm Section

Also by William Drennan:

The Fourth Strike:
Hiring and Training the Disadvantaged
(editor)

Cover design by ABA Publishing.

Printed in the United States of America.

09 08 07 06 05 5 4 3 2 1

Library of Congress Cataloging-in-Publication Data

Drennan, William
    Advocacy words a thesaurus.
    William Drennan
Library of Congress Cataloging-in-Publication Data is on file.

ISBN 1-59031-528-6

In memory of my father

Contents

Preface

Effective word use is vital for anyone active in the law. For
the attorney arguing a case or preparing a brief, for the jurist
writing an opinion, even for the law student, words are
the ammunition needed to make the point. For example,
in attacking the credibility of opposing counsel's witness, a
litigator might use such devastatingly critical terms as *cowardly*
for prudent; *disdainful* or *haughty* for proud; *indifferent*
or *lazy* for easygoing; *brash* or *vicious* for assertive; *coerce,
intimidate,* or *con* for persuade; *plot* for plan; *irresponsible*
for uninhibited; *hasty* for swift; and *dream up* for formulate.
These and other persuasive words are available to you—
quickly—in the pages that follow.

Now anyone in the legal profession can use the same
words that advocacy journalists use to make their point so
effectively. *Advocacy Words: A Thesaurus* gives them to you in
an easy-to-use format. The words are arranged alphabetically in
two groups: favorable-critical (Part One) and critical-favorable
(Part Two). You need only look in one column and see the
corresponding advocacy word or words in the opposite
column—there are no cross-references.

Let *Advocacy Words* be your companion in painting
the verbal picture you want. Keep it handy to help you move
others to your point of view.

Acknowledgments

My thanks particularly to two people in putting this book into print and published:

To Richard G. Paszkiet, executive editor at ABA Book Publishing, who believed in this project from the outset and who expertly guided it to publication.

To my wife, Christina, who does all my typing, often into the wee hours, and who very competently transferred the manuscript onto compact disc and hard copy.

Part One

Favorable-Critical

Favorable	**Critical**
absorption	takeover
accept (an argument)	buy (an argument), give in to
accidental	deliberate, intentional
accommodation	appeasement, giving in
accomplish	finagle, engineer, pull off
accurate	lucky
accuse	slur
achieve	finagle, engineer, pull off
acquisition	takeover
actively support	incite, harangue, whip up
ad	hype, plug, push, self-serving document
adage	cliché, hackneyed expression
adamant	stubborn, inflexible, obstinate, pigheaded
address	get around to
adherence to tradition	business as usual
adjust	correct, fix, fiddle with
adjustment	extra charge
administration	regime, ruling circles, ruling clique
Administration, the	the Bush Administration

Favorable	**Critical**
advance on	chase, pursue, invade, infiltrate
advance to the rear	turn tail, be routed, run, flee, panic, run in panic
advertisement	self-serving document
advertising	propaganda
adviser	crony, pal
advocacy	bias, propaganda
advocate	propagandist, apologist, mouthpiece, lobbyist
aesthete	fop, dilettante
affirmative action	reverse racism, preferential hiring for minorities
afflicted	crippled
aged and infirm	senile, dotty
aggressive	predatory
agreeable	manipulable, docile, meek, pliant, compliant, collaborative, toadying
agreement	conspiracy, deal
aid (v.)	prop up, buttress, collaborate with
air support	bombing

Favorable	**Critical**
airy	frivolous, trivial
alarmed	frightened, afraid, panicky
alcoholic	drunk
alert (adj.)	nervous, hyper
alert (v.)	alarm, jar, startle
alliance	clique, gang, cartel, cabal
all-white	lily-white
alternate	weird, strange, bizarre, off the wall, twisted, perverse, queer, hippie, warped, gross
alternating	erratic, seesawing, vacillating
altruistic	masochistic
analysis	opinion, rationalization, hocus-pocus, diatribe
and	but
annexation	takeover, conquest
anonymous	secret, hidden, concealed, in hiding
anxiety neurosis	cowardice
anxious	panicky, desperate, frantic
apparatus	contraption
appeal	hype, sell, push, hustle, preach, peddle, pitch, promote, hawk

Favorable	**Critical**
appetite	greed, avarice
apply	smear on
appointed, be	seize power, come to power
appraisal	guess
apprehensive	panicky, desperate, frantic
apprentice	incompetent, inexperienced, raw
approach	scheme, ploy, tactic, plot, gambit, maneuver, device
argue	quibble, nit-pick
argue a fine point	quibble, nit-pick
armed revolutionary	terrorist
aroused	hysterical, intemperate, frenzied, out of control
arrange	pile, heap
arrangement	conspiracy, deal
arrived in	hit
artist	graffiti painter
ask for	agitate for, demand
assemble	swarm
assert	allege, claim, charge, mouth
assert forcefully	rant, scream, harangue

Favorable	Critical
assertive	arrogant, aggressive, cocky, brash, pushy, feisty, threatening, strident, tyrannical, arbitrary, brutal, strong-arm, bullying, vicious
assertive leader	demagogue, tyrant, despot, dictator
assertive spokesperson	agitator, loudmouth, nuisance, pest, a bother
assist	prop up, buttress, collaborate with
associate	crony, pal
association	clique, gang, cartel, cabal
assume office	seize power, come to power
at one's choice	arbitrary
attack	slur, libel, slander, demean, smear
attend to	be bothered with
attorney	mouthpiece
authoritarian	totalitarian, tyrannical
avenge	get even for, counterhit
avoidance	haughtiness, disdain

Favorable	Critical
backer	propagandist, apologist, mouthpiece, lobbyist
bargain	conspiracy, deal, rip-off
basic	primal
beachcomber	vagrant, bum, ne'er-do-well
be in charge	rule the roost
beliefs	doctrines, rules, dogma
bend the truth	lie, fabricate
bold	arrogant, aggressive, brash
bop	hit, strike
born out of wedlock	bastard, illegitimate
brief (adj.)	superficial, sketchy
brief (v.)	pitch, propagandize, try to sell to, hype, plug
bright	wily, clever, cagey, cunning, shrewd, sly, slick, shifty
bring group pressure	gang up
bring to justice	persecute
bring to one's attention	badger, bait, intimidate, bully, harass, agitate, hector
bucolic environment or areas	the sticks
budget	cheap, shoddy

Favorable	Critical
bulletin	rag, sheet, filthy sheet
burly	bloated, fat, blimpy, lardlike, beefy, flabby, bulky
business	racket, scam, con
businessman	profiteer, exploiter, imperialist
busing	forced busing
by the book	cold, pompous, frigid, frosty, stuffed shirt, haughty, aloof, rigid, inflexible
called	branded, labeled
campaign	road show, dog and pony show
candid	in bad taste, disgusting, repulsive
capitalist	profiteer, exploiter, imperialist
capitulate	give up, go belly up, throw in the towel
careful	suspicious, paranoid, uncertain, fussy, nit-picking, prissy, mincing, timid, gun-shy, scared, frightened, fearful, cowardly, compromising, lacking in principle

Favorable	**Critical**
careful with money	tightfisted, stingy, miserly
casual	sloppy, motley, ragtag, scruffy, disorganized, ratty, dirty, filthy, slovenly, careless, messy, frivolous, backdoor
cater to	pander to, coddle, indulge
Caucasian	lily-white
cautious	fussy, nit-picking, prissy, suspicious, paranoiac, mincing, timid, gun-shy, scared, frightened, fearful, cowardly
central authority	dictatorship, tyranny
ceremony	hocus-pocus, circus
champion	propagandist, apologist, mouthpiece, lobbyist
chance	speculation, gamble
change allegiance	betray
characterized by	riddled with, swarming with, infested with
charge (v.)	slur, libel, slander, demean, blame
charismatic leader	demagogue, tyrant, despot
chastise	beat, flail, whip
chunky	squat, pudgy

Favorable	Critical
circulate	run around
circumspect	fussy, nit-picking, prissy, fearful, overcautious
classic	typical, old
clear	naive, simpleminded, obvious, transparent
clergyman	religionist, preacher
clue	rumor, gossip
coincidental	deliberate
colleague	crony, pal, collaborator
collect	rake in, scrape up
combat fatigue	cowardice
combat team	death squad
comfort	mollify, appease
comment on	mock, deride, ridicule
commercial	hype
community group	gang, cult, mob, crowd, swarm, clique, lot
community organization	gang, cult, mob, crowd, swarm, clique, lot
compact	squat, pudgy
compassionate	soft, lax, indulgent

Favorable	**Critical**
complain	fulminate against, whine, gripe
complaint	tirade, jeremiad, rant
complex	jumbled, confusing, convoluted
compromise (v.)	give in, back down
concealed	underhanded, sneaky, dishonest, hidden, smuggled, disguised
conceive	cook up, dream up, concoct
concentrate on	be obsessed with
concerned	alarmed, worried, panicky, desperate, frantic
confederation	clique, gang, cartel, cabal
confident	cocky, egotistical, arrogant
confidential	covered up, clandestine, secret
confront	slur, libel, slander, demean
congregate	swarm
conservative	reactionary, obsolete, old-fashioned
considered judgment	guess, hunch
considering alternate opinions	confused, indecisive

Favorable	Critical
consistent	static, repetitive, rigid
consolidate	pick up the pieces, lump together
consortium	clique, gang, cartel, cabal
contract	conspiracy, deal
contribute	be deprived of
contribute to	throw at
contribution	two cents' worth
controversial	infamous, notorious
convenient	gets around (something), easier, propitious, expedient
convert	con, talk (one) into, proselytize, hype, sell, push, hustle, preach, peddle, pitch, promote, hawk, coerce, muscle, force, dragoon, strong-arm, intimidate, coerce
convince	hype, sell, push, hustle, preach, peddle, pitch, promote, hawk, con, talk (one) into, proselytize, coerce, muscle, force, dragoon, strong-arm, intimidate, coerce
cooperate with	collaborate with

Favorable	Critical
cooperative	manipulable, docile, meek, pliant, compliant, collaborative, toadying
coordination	coincidence
correct	cold, pompous, rigid, frosty, stuffed shirt, aloof, frigid, self-righteous
council	regime, ruling circles, ruling clique
courageous	desperate, frantic, foolhardy, impetuous
covering organization	front
covert	sneaky, underhanded
creative	radical, flighty, undisciplined
creative ambiguity	doubletalk, gibberish, nonsense
creativity	fantasy, whim
critical	derisive, scornful, scalding, withering, scathing
critical examination	hatchet job
criticism	diatribe, censure, denigration
critique	mock, deride, criticize
crowd	mob, rabble, swarm, horde

Favorable	Critical
dashing	impulsive, foolhardy, showy
dean	oldest member
debate	quibble, nit-pick, argue, bicker
debate-minded	contentious, combative, belligerent
decisive	tyrannical, arbitrary, brutal, strong-arm, bullying, vicious
decisively	trampling, running roughshod over
declare	allege, claim, mouth, pipe up, spout
dedicated	extremist, fanatic, crank, wild, mad dog, workaholic, ambitious
defiant	insubordinate, mutinous
delay	stop cold, hinder, obstruct
deliberate	tedious, slow, uncertain
delicate	mincing, weak, flimsy
delightfully cramped	cluttered
deliver	scrape up
demonstrate	harangue, riot
demonstration leader	rabble-rouser, agitator
demonstrator	agitator, loudmouth, dissident

Favorable	Critical
deposit	dump, unload
destiny of a people	insurrection, rebellion, terrorism, invasion, occupation
determination	guess, hunch
determined	stubborn, obstinate, brutal, vicious, savage, intractable
developing	backward, underdeveloped
device	contraption
devise	cook up
diet	malnutrition, hunger, famine
different	weird, strange, bizarre, off the wall, twisted, perverse, queer, disadvantaged
dignified	cold, pompous, frigid, frosty, stuffed shirt, haughty, aloof, condescending, contemptuous
direct (adj.)	naive, childish, simpleminded, crude
direct (v.)	force, order, dictate, boss
direction	dictation, preachment
disabled	crippled
discharge	fire, kick out, can, boot out

Favorable	**Critical**
discipline (n.)	regimentation
discipline (v.)	beat
discontinue	fire
discounted	cheap, shoddy
discretionary	arbitrary
disparate	hodgepodge, messy, jumbled, in disarray, a collection, scattered
dispatch with	murder, butcher, annihilate, slaughter, assassinate
displaced homemaker	divorcée
display	flaunt
distinguished	infamous, notorious
distinguished by	infested with, swarming with
diverse	hodgepodge, messy, jumbled, in disarray, a collection, disparate, contradictory, deviant
diversified experience, one with	journeyman
document (v.)	claim
dogged	plodding
doing	up to
dominant leader	boss, strongman

Favorable	Critical
down on his luck	bum, loser
dynamic	unstable, speculative, insecure
dynamic leader	demagogue, tyrant, despot
eager for combat	bloodthirsty, savage
eager to engage the enemy	bloodthirsty, savage, spoiling for a fight
earnest	pious, self-righteous
earnestly desire	slaver after, lust for, crave
earthy	disgusting, obscene
easygoing	indifferent, cavalier, casual, offhand, lazy, slothful, weak, soft, permissive
eccentric	weird, strange, bizarre, off the wall, twisted, perverse, queer, hippie, warped, gross, peculiar, outlandish
eclectic	hodgepodge, messy, jumbled, in disarray, a collection
economical	shabby
educate	hype, sell, push, hustle, preach, peddle, pitch, promote, hawk, brainwash
educator	teacher

Favorable	Critical
effervescent	unstable, hyper
efficient	curt, rude, short, abrupt
efficient political organization	machine
elected, be	seize power, come to power
emergency (adj.)	reckless, hasty
emerging	backward, underdeveloped
employees	mercenaries, hirelings, hired hands, hired guns, henchmen
encounter (v.)	run across, stumble on
encourage	incite, harangue, whip up, egg on
energetic	extremist, fanatical, crank, wild, mad dog
energetic disassembly	explosion
enforcement detachment	goon squad, muscle
engaged in	up to
enlarged	bloated, huge, enormous, gigantic
enormous self-esteem	egomania, cockiness
enter	intrude into, encroach on
enterprise	racket, scheme, swindle, con

Favorable	Critical
enthusiastic	impetuous, gullible
entrepreneur	profiteer, exploiter, imperialist
erroneous	boneheaded, stupid, knuckleheaded, nonsensical, idiotic, imbecilic, moronic
espouse	agitate for
estimate	guess, opinion, stab in the dark
ethnically diverse	mongrel, mutt
evaluate	criticize
evasion	lie
event	accident, mishap
even-tempered	permissive, weak
evidence	opinion, propaganda, indoctrination, brainwashing, rumor, hearsay, libel, slander
exact (v.)	strip (v.), deprive, wrest from
examine	spy on, snoop on, peer at, bother
example	straw man
example (of a person)	specimen (of a person)
excess	garbage, trash, rubbish, glut

Favorable	Critical
exciting	unstable, speculative, insecure
exclude	fire, kick out, can, boot out, throw out
exclusive	monopoly
execute	murder, butcher, annihilate, slaughter, assassinate
exhort	incite, harangue, whip up
expansive	bloated, huge, enormous, gigantic, inflated, monstrous
expel	kick out, throw out, banish
experienced	over the hill, old, ancient, decadent, obsolete, outdated, elderly, has-been, washed up, worn out, old-line, old-fashioned, creaking
explain	hype, sell, push, hustle, preach, peddle, pitch, promote, hawk
explanation	excuse, rationalization
explosives expert	bomber
explosives technician	bomber
export	dump
expose	persecute, defame, besmirch
exposé	smear

Favorable	**Critical**
expound	hype, sell, push, hustle, preach, peddle, pitch, promote, hawk, spout
express (v.)	flaunt
express intention	promise
extrovert	back-slapper, hail fellow well met
fact	opinion, propaganda, indoctrination, brainwashing, rumor, hearsay, libel, slander
fall back	turn tail, be routed, run, flee, panic, run in panic, run out, quit
famous	infamous, notorious
fashion industry	rag trade
fastidious	fussy, nit-picking, prissy
favoring	biased, slanted, prejudiced
fence-sitting	hypocritical, insensitive, coldhearted, indecisive, indifferent
financially cautious	tightfisted, stingy, miserly
financially conservative	tightfisted, stingy, miserly
firm advocate	hard-liner

Favorable	Critical
firm rule	dictatorship, tyranny, despotism
flexible	hypocritical, insensitive, coldhearted, erratic, irregular, wishy-washy, indecisive
flexible negotiator	soft-liner, appeaser
focus on	be obsessed with
folk belief	myth, old wives' tale, superstition
folk wisdom	myth, old wives' tale, superstition
follow	eat the dust of, trail behind, follow the lead of, take directions from, chase, chase after, run after, pursue
forceful	arrogant, aggressive, vicious, savage, brutal, cruel, heavy-handed, strident
forceful language	diatribe, billingsgate, tirade
forcefully	trampling, running roughshod over
forces	lackeys, minions
foresighted	cunning, clever, shrewd
forewarn	alarm

Favorable	Critical
formal	cold, pompous, stuffy, frigid, frosty, stuffed-shirt, rigid, haughty, aloof, conceited
formula	scheme, notion, plot
formulate	cook up, dream up, concoct, make up
forthright	blunt, crude, insensitive, aggressive, threatening, in bad taste, repulsive, disgusting
fortified	propped up
fortunate	lucky
frank	blunt, crude, insensitive, aggressive, threatening, in bad taste, repulsive, disgusting
frank discussion	argument
frank exchange of ideas	argument
frantic	hysterical, panicky
freedom	license, anarchy, running wild
freedom fighter	terrorist
freelance	self-styled, isolated, insular, lone
friends	cronies, henchmen

Favorable	Critical
frugal	pennypinching, cheap, tight, stingy, greedy, miserly
full	bloated, huge, enormous, gigantic, engorged, jaded, dissipated
full-figured	bloated, fat, blimpy, lardlike, beefy, flabby, bulky, huge, enormous, gigantic
gained by	lost to (another party)
garment industry	rag trade
garner	scrape up
gather	rake in, scrape up
generous	bloated, huge, inflated, monstrous, excessive
gentleman	guy, man, male, dandy
give	supply
glamorous	flashy, gaudy, ostentatious
glittering	flashy, gaudy, ostentatious
golden-ager	old man, old woman
good fortune	luck, accident
good judgment	lucky guess, accident
government	regime, ruling circles, ruling clique

Favorable	Critical
gracious	condescending, haughty, contemptuous
graciously	condescendingly, stoopingly
grim	morbid
group	gang, cult, mob, crowd, swarm, clique, horde, lot, cartel, cabal, rabble, breed
guerrilla	terrorist
guide (n.)	preachment
guide (v.)	shove, push, control, pressure
hairpiece	rug
handicapped	crippled
handle	get around to
happen upon	blunder into, stumble on
hardheaded	insensitive, coldhearted
hard worker	workaholic, fanatic
has many contributing elements	hodgepodge, messy, jumbled, in disarray, a collection
has potential	amateur, inexperienced, untried
headquarters	lair, hideout

Favorable	Critical
heavy-set	bloated, fat, blimpy, lardlike, beefy, flabby, bulky
help	prop up, buttress, collaborate with
help financially	fill the coffers, funnel money to
heroic	foolhardy, impetuous
heterogeneous	hodgepodge, messy, jumbled, in disarray, a collection
hidden	sneaky
highly effective	dangerous
holding firm	stubborn, inflexible
home	house
home base	lair, hideout
home grounds	lair, hideout
honest	gullible, naive, susceptible
human being	animal
human services	welfare, relief
hysteria	cowardice
illustration	straw man
imagination	fantasy
implement (n.)	contraption, gadget

Favorable	Critical
implement a death sentence of	murder, butcher, annihilate, slaughter, assassinate
implementer	enforcer, hatchet man, hit man
imprecise	boneheaded, stupid, knuckleheaded, nonsensical, idiotic, imbecilic, moronic, vague
impromptu	accidental
incident	disaster, catastrophe
inclined toward	biased, slanted, prejudiced
incomplete success	failure
incorrect	absurd, ridiculous
increased	bloated, huge, inflated, monstrous
independent	insubordinate, self-styled, isolated, insular, lone
independent contractor	journeyman
independent worker	strikebreaker, scab
indication	rumor, gossip
indigenous	native
indiscreet	gross, crude, rash
individual choice	whim, caprice, impulse

Favorable	Critical
industrialist	profiteer, exploiter, imperialist
inebriated	drunk, besotted
ineffective	exploited, powerless, impotent
in error	stupid, dumb, moronic, idiotic, imbecilic
inexpensive	cheap, shoddy, inferior, shabby
influence	coerce, arm-twist, have a grip on
in flux	disorganized, chaotic, confused
inform	hype, sell, push, hustle, preach, peddle, pitch, promote, hawk
informal	sloppy, motley, ragtag, scruffy, disorganized, ratty, dirty, filthy, slovenly, careless, messy, chaotic, disorderly, indifferent, cavalier, offhand, casual, lazy, slothful, haphazard, backdoor
informal contribution	bribe, payoff
informally prepared	shoddy, sloppy

Favorable	Critical
information	opinion, propaganda, indoctrination, brainwashing, rumor, hearsay, libel, slander
in no hurry	late, delinquent
in private practice	self-styled, isolated, insular, lone
in reserve	hidden, kept secret, concealed
in righteous indignation	with a snarl, with a scowl
insistent	stubborn, obstinate, intractable
inspiration	lucky guess, blind guess, stab in the dark, jaundiced view, stumbling into
inspire	egg on, incite
instance	straw man
instruct	order
instruction	preachment
intelligence agent	spy, mole, infiltrator
intelligence operative	spy, mole, infiltrator
intelligent	wily, clever, cagey, cunning, shrewd, sly, slick, shifty
interpose	interrupt, intrude, butt in

Favorable	**Critical**
in transition	disorganized, chaotic, confused
intricate	jumbled, confusing
introduce	trot out
introspective	moody, brooding
inveigh against	rail against
inventor	crackpot, tinkerer
investigate	spy on, snoop on, peer at, harass, snipe at, bother, annoy
involvement	meddling, interference
irregular	sloppy, motley, ragtag, scruffy, disorganized, ratty, dirty, filthy, slovenly, careless, messy, erratic, capricious, bizarre, hodgepodge, aimless
irregularly featured	disfigured, ugly
irregular warrior	terrorist
issue-oriented organization	pressure group
jest	crack
joke	crack
journal	rag, sheet, filthy sheet

Favorable	Critical
journalism	muckraking, editorializing
journalist	self-styled writer
journey	junket
judgment	guess, opinion, stab in the dark, error, malpractice
justice-seeking	vindictive, vengeful
keep from view	hide, smuggle, sneak
kill	murder, butcher, annihilate, slaughter, assassinate, massacre
lacking adequate defense	sitting duck
lady	bitch, woman, female
large	bloated, huge, enormous, gigantic, massive
lawyer	mouthpiece
lay	dump
lay down	dump
lay off	fire
lead	dictate, boss, dominate
league	clique, gang, cartel, cabal

Favorable / Critical

Favorable	Critical
learning	incompetent, inexperienced
leave	abandon, get out of
Lebensraum	invasion, occupation
legislate	push through
legislator	politician
leisurely	indifferently, cavalierly, casually, offhandedly, lazily, slothfully, tediously, slowly
liberal	radical
liberation	occupation, capture, fall, overrunning
liberators	invaders, terrorists
liberty	license, anarchy, running wild
lift one's voice	scream, shout, yell, bellow, shriek
light	frivolous
list	rogues' gallery
living together	affair
load	pile
local	native
local inhabitant	native
love child	bastard, illegitimate
loyalty	obsequiousness, fealty

Favorable	Critical
machine	contraption
maintain	charge, accuse
make	rake in
manage	dictate, boss
mandate	force, order
manifest destiny	invasion, occupation, insurrection, rebellion, terrorism
man-made	artificial
manufacture	grind out, churn out, crank out
manufacturer	profiteer, exploiter, imperialist
many successes	a spotty record
matriarchal	old woman, over the hill, old, ancient, decadent, obsolete, outdated, elderly, has-been, washed up, worn out, old-line, old-fashioned, creaking, rickety
maverick	insubordinate, outlaw
meaningful	ominous
mentally disturbed	crazy, insane, nutty, psychotic, loony, out of one's mind, lunatic, mad, raving

Favorable	Critical
mentally ill	crazy, insane, nutty, psychotic, loony, out of one's mind, lunatic, mad, raving
merchant	huckster, profiteer, exploiter, imperialist
message	hype, promotion, propaganda
method	scheme, ploy, tactic, plot, gambit, maneuver, device
middle-of-the-road	straddling the fence
militant	extremist, fanatic, crank, wild, mad dog
military adviser	participant, warmonger
miraculous	tricky
miscellaneous	hodgepodge, messy, jumbled, in disarray, a collection of
miscellaneous items	junk
mistaken	boneheaded, stupid, knuckleheaded, nonsensical, idiotic, imbecilic, moronic, dumb
mixed	hodgepodge, messy, jumbled, in disarray, a collection of
modify	hedge
money	loot

Favorable	**Critical**
monitor	spy on, stalk, harass, bother, pester
moral	impractical, lofty, noble
more than	less than (in greater amount)
mother country	colonial power
move (n.)	tactic
move (v.)	shove, push
move after	chase, pursue
move deliberately	straggle, lag
move decisively	ram through
move heavily	lumber
move into	invade
move on	drift
move slowly	straggle, lag
move stealthily	sneak, slink
moving	maudlin, tear-jerking, mawkish
muscle	brawn
mutual plan of action	conspiracy, deal, scheme

Favorable	Critical
named	called
name or term alone	name or term preceded by "so-called"
name preceded by title	name alone
national security	special interests
necessary	illegal, immoral, expedient
need	want
needing repair	dilapidated, run-down
negritude	black racism
news	opinion, propaganda, indoctrination, brainwashing, rumor, hearsay, libel, slander
news coverage	publicity blitz
newspaper	rag, sheet, filthy sheet
nimble	wily, clever, cagey, cunning, shrewd, sly, slick, shifty
no holds barred	savage, vicious
not accept	turn down, refuse
noted	infamous, notorious, blatant, grandiose, brazen
not fully sophisticated	boorish, crude, rude
not quite accurate	boneheaded, stupid, knuckleheaded, nonsensical, idiotic, imbecilic, moronic

Favorable	Critical
nudge	alarm, jar
number of people	head count
obese	bloated, fat, blimpy, lardlike, beefy, flabby, bulky
observe	claim, spy on
obvious	blatant
occurrence	disaster
off-balance	clumsy
offbeat	weird, strange, bizarre, off the wall, twisted, perverse, queer, hippie, warped, gross
official	strongman's crony
off-target	boneheaded, stupid, knuckleheaded, nonsensical, idiotic, imbecilic, moronic
off-the-mark	boneheaded, stupid, knuckleheaded, nonsensical, idiotic, imbecilic, moronic
one of a kind	strange, odd, irregular, offbeat, bizarre
opponent	enemy
opportunistic	accidental

Favorable	Critical
opposition	reaction
optimistic projections	pie in the sky
organization	gang, cult, mob, crowd, swarm, clique
oust	fire, kick out, can, boot out, throw out
outgoing person	back-slapper, hail fellow well met
outreach	tentacles
outside chance	speculation, gamble
outside the law	criminal, illegal
outspoken	loud, noisy
outstanding	blatant, grandiose
over	only (for amount to be deemphasized)
overpowering	lethal, vicious, savage
overwhelming	lethal, vicious, savage
own variety of	fake, counterfeit, artificial
pacing oneself	indifferent, cavalier, casual, offhand, lazy, slothful

Favorable	**Critical**
pact	conspiracy, deal
pale	pasty-faced
parsimonious	tightfisted, stingy, miserly
pass	push through
pass up	ignore
patriarchal	old man, over the hill, old, ancient, decadent, obsolete, outdated, elderly, has-been, washed up, worn out, old-line, old-fashioned, creaking, rickety
patrol	prowl
pay	be deprived of
peaceful	dead slow, dreary, slow, boring, lethargic
people	lot, gang
perceptive	cunning, clever, shrewd
performance	act, show, song-and-dance act, dog and pony show
persistent	stubborn, plodding
person	animal
perspicacious	timid, fearful, cowardly, compromising, lacking in principle, cunning, clever, shrewd

Favorable	Critical
persuade	hype, sell, push, hustle, preach, peddle, pitch, promote, hawk, con, talk (one) into, coerce, intimidate, muscle, force, dragoon, strong-arm
petition	agitate for, demand
philosopher	dreamer
phrase laundering	lying
place (n.)	joint, dump
place (v.)	dump, toss
place down	dump
plan (n.)	scheme, ploy, tactic, plot, gambit, maneuver, device, notion, connivance
plan (v.)	concoct, engineer, manipulate
poignant	maudlin, tear-jerking, mawkish
point with pride	brag, boast, gloat
poised	cocky
political figure	politician
polyglot	jumble
popular belief	myth, old wives' tale, superstition

Favorable	Critical
popular democracy	mob rule
popular expression	cliché, catchword, slogan, catchphrase
popular wisdom	myth, old wives' tale, superstition
portion	glop
portly	bloated, fat, blimpy, lardlike, beefy, flabby, bulky
position paper	tract, sheet
possibility	speculation, gamble
possibly	suspiciously
postpone	stop cold
potent	lethal, vicious, savage, dangerous
practical	hypocritical, insensitive, coldhearted
practical joke	trick
pragmatic	hypocritical, insensitive, coldhearted, timid, fearful, cowardly, compromising, lacking in principle
precise	fussy, nit-picking, prissy
precise expressions	jargon, gibberish

Favorable	Critical
prediction	lucky guess, blind guess, stab in the dark, jaundiced view, stumbling into
prefer	fancy
preferred	pet
prepare	concoct, make up
prescient	cunning, clever, shrewd
present (v.)	hype, sell, push, hustle, preach, peddle, pitch, promote, hawk, trot out
presentation	act, show, song-and-dance act
present to	throw at
preserve	prop up
President, the	Bush
President Bush	Bush
pressure	intimidation, fear, arm-twisting, putting the screws to
preventive detention	imprisonment
previously owned	used
prickly	stubborn, inflexible
pride	ego
prim	mincing

Favorable	Critical
principled	stubborn, inflexible, impractical, lofty, noble
principles	platitudes, slogans, doctrines, rules, dogma
priority	special privilege
private	privileged, segregated
privileged	covered up, clandestine, secret
probably	suspiciously
probe	bother
proceed cautiously	pussyfoot
proceeding	hocus-pocus
proclaim	allege, claim, mouth, spout
procure	pick up
prod	agitate, annoy
produce	grind out, crank out, trot out
program	scheme, notion, plot
progressive	radical
prominent	notorious
promotion	hype, plug, self-serving document
proper	stuffy
propose	toss out

Favorable	Critical
protagonist	hatchetman
protective custody	imprisonment
protest (n.)	tirade, jeremiad
protest (v.)	whine, complain, have a chip on one's shoulder
protest demonstration	disturbance, mob scene, riot
protester	agitator, loudmouth
proud	egotistical, arrogant, vain, *macho*, scornful, supercilious, sneering, disdainful, haughty, vain
prudent	timid, fearful, cowardly, compromising, lacking in principle, gun-shy, paranoid
publication	tract, sheet, rag
public official	politician
public opinion	propaganda
pursue	chase after, run after, stalk
put	dump, toss
put down	dump
put under surveillance	spy on

Favorable	Critical
qualify	hedge
quick	impetuous, hasty, hurried, ill-conceived, desperate
quiet	dead slow, dreary, slow, boring
racial pride	racism
raise one's voice	scream, shout, yell, bellow, shriek
rally (v.)	harangue
rapid oxidation	fire
reason	excuse, alibi
reassure	mollify
receipts	take
recipients	outstretched palms
redeploy	turn tail, be routed, run, flee, panic, run in panic
reduce the population of	murder, butcher, annihilate, slaughter, assassinate, decimate
regroup	pick up the pieces
regular	humdrum, boring, repetitious
regulator	enforcer

Favorable	Critical
relationship	affair
relaxed	permissive, weak
reliable	stodgy
remind	badger, bait, intimidate, bully, harass, agitate, hector, nag
remove	kidnap, steal
remove from office	impeach, depose
reparations	loot
report (n.)	rumor, gossip, hearsay
report (v.)	allege, claim, mouth, accuse
request	agitate for, demand
require	force, make
reserve	deny
resident	native
resign	run out, quit
resolute	inflexible
resort	playground
responded forcefully	shot back
restful	dead slow, dreary, slow, boring
restrain	restrict
restraint projectile	bullet

Favorable	Critical
retain	hide, smuggle, sneak
retaliate	flail back, get even
retarded	stupid, dumb, moronic, idiotic, imbecilic
retreat	turn tail, be routed, run, flee, panic, run in panic, run out, quit
retreat in an orderly way	turn tail, be routed, run, flee, panic, run in panic, run out, quit
returned funds	kickback
reveal	allege
revenue	loot
revered belief	myth, old wives' tale, superstition, fairy tale
revered wisdom	myth, old wives' tale, superstition, fairy tale
revise	correct, fix
revise one's position	do an about-face
revolution	rebellion, mutiny, insurrection
rite	hocus-pocus
ritual	hocus-pocus
rock-ribbed	inflexible, rigid

Favorable	Critical
routine	tedious, boring, dreary
rugged	lined, dirty
rugged-featured	scarred, deformed, acne-scarred
rural environment or areas	the sticks
rustic environment or areas	the sticks
rustic person	hick, country bumpkin, boor, hayseed, redneck
salesperson	huckster
same reason	same old song
satiated	bloated, jaded, dissipated, engorged, glutted
satisfied	bloated, jaded, dissipated, engorged, glutted
save	prop up
say	claim, charge, allege, mouth, spout
seasoned	over the hill, old, ancient, decadent, obsolete, outdated, elderly, has-been, washed up, worn out, old-line, old-fashioned, creaking, rickety, old man, old woman

Favorable	Critical
secluded	holed up
Second World	Communist, slave state, Commie
secret (v.)	hide, conceal
secure (adj.)	stodgy, boring, dreary
secure (v.)	engineer, pick up
security-conscious	suspicious, paranoiac, neurotic
seek	chase after, run after
seek safety	run away, cower
seize	grab
selected	pet
selective	narrow
self-assured	conceited
self-confident	arrogant, aggressive, cocky, brash
self-employed	self-styled, isolated, insular, lone
self-esteem	conceit, ego
self-possessed	conceited
self-sacrificing	masochistic
senator	junior senator

Favorable	Critical
senior	over the hill, old, ancient, decadent, obsolete, outdated, elderly, has-been, washed up, worn out, old-line, old-fashioned, creaking, rickety, old man, old woman
senior senator	senator
sensation	scandal
separate neighborhood	ghetto
serious	stodgy, boring, dreary
served	spent time
set forth	hype, sell, push, hustle, preach, peddle, pitch, promote, hawk, spout
several tries	repeated bunglings
sexual convenience center	brothel, whorehouse
sexual explicitness	smut, pornography, filth
sexually active	promiscuous, oversexed, horny
sexually frank	obscene, tawdry, filthy
sexual preference	sexual perversion, sexual deviation, sexual queerness
sexual realism	smut, pornography, filth

Favorable	Critical
sharing quarters	affair
shell shock	cowardice
shelter	flophouse
shift allegiance	betray
ship (v.)	dump
shore up	prop up
show (v.)	allege
simple	naive, simpleminded
sincere	gullible, naive, pious
singularly featured	disfigured, ugly
skilled	lucky
slacken one's hand	lose control
slight	skinny
small-arms expert	gunner
small-arms technician	gunner
small group	handful
smart	wily, clever, cagey, cunning, shrewd, sly, slick, shifty
smooth-running political organization	machine
snake-bitten	incompetent
socialist	Communist, slave state, Commie

Favorable	Critical
socialize	run around
social transfer payments	welfare, relief
soldier	butcher, killer, murderer
solid	inflexible, rigid
solution	nostrum
somewhat overdue	late, delinquent
sophisticated	affected
sound	cunning, clever, shrewd
speak about	allege, claim, mouth, accuse
speak out	pipe up
speak out about	allege, claim, mouth, accuse
speak softly	mumble, mutter
special	strange, odd, irregular, offbeat, bizarre, different, retarded
specialization	narrow interest
specialized language	jargon, gibberish
special services	welfare, relief
spokesperson	propagandist, mouthpiece, apologist, lobbyist, PR person
spontaneously	out of left field, accidentally
spread (v.)	glop

Favorable	Critical
stable	stodgy, boring, dreary, stagnant
stable income	fixed income
stack	pile
standardized	tedious, boring, dreary
star-crossed	incompetent
state (n.)	regime, ruling circles, ruling clique
state (v.)	allege, claim, mouth, spout, charge
stately	cold, contemptuous
statement	utterance
statesman	politician
steer	shove, control
stern	vicious, savage, brutal
sticking by one's guns	stubborn, inflexible
stout	bloated, fat, blimpy, lardlike, beefy, flabby, bulky
straggler	deserter
straightforward	naive, childish, simpleminded, crude
strategic retreat	backing down, appeasement, giving in

Favorable	Critical
strategic withdrawal	backing down, appeasement, giving in
strategy	scheme, ploy, tactic, plot, gambit, maneuver, device, gimmick, trick
street politics	gutter politics
strike	punch, clout, beat, thump, pound
strike with emphasis	punch, clout, beat, thump, pound
striking	blatant
strong	tyrannical, arbitrary, brutal, strong-arm, bullying, vicious, egotistical, heavy-handed
strongly worded	intemperate, provocative
strong-willed	egotistical
struggle (v.)	lash out
student	attendee
study	spy on
subordinate (adj.)	inferior, lower, lesser
subordinate (n.)	lackey, puppet, flunky, yes-man, toady, sycophant, truckler
subsidize	prop up, buttress

Favorable	Critical
substantial	bloated, huge, inflated, monstrous, massive, severe
summary	superficial
support	prop up, buttress
supporter	lackey, puppet, flunky, yes-man, toady, sycophant, truckler, pal, handmaiden
surplus	garbage, trash, rubbish
surprise offensive	sneak attack, ambush
surrender	give up, go belly up, throw in the towel
suspicious	paranoid
swift	hasty, hurried, desperate
swing	swipe
symbols	trappings
systematic	regimented, inflexible, stiff
tactical retreat	backing down, appeasement, giving in
tactical withdrawal	backing down, appeasement, giving in
take	kidnap, steal
take the reins of government	seize power, come to power

Favorable	Critical
take up residence in	invade, infiltrate
temporarily standing	loitering
temporary resident	vagrant, bum
termed	branded, labeled
terminate	fire, kick out, can, boot out
theoretical	dubious, guesswork
thin	skinny, bony
thorough	fussy, nit-picking, prissy
thought to help by	got the idea of
thrifty	pennypinching, cheap, tight, greedy
time-honored	over the hill, old, ancient, decadent, obsolete, outdated, elderly, has-been, washed up, worn out, old-line, old-fashioned, creaking, rickety
time-tested	over the hill, old, ancient, decadent, obsolete, outdated, elderly, has-been, washed up, worn out, old-line, old-fashioned, creaking, rickety
time-tested expression	cliché, catchword, slogan, catchphrase
title followed by first name	first name only, last name only

Favorable	Critical
title followed by last name	first name only, last name only
title only	title preceded by "self-styled"
tough	tyrannical, arbitrary, brutal, strong-arm, bullying, vicious, savage
tradition	old hat, old practice
traditional	reactionary, obsolete, hidebound, set in one's ways
traditional belief	myth, old wives' tale, superstition
traditional wisdom	myth, old wives' tale, superstition
tragedy	disgrace
tragic person	degenerate, crook, thief
tranquil	dead slow, dreary, slow, boring
transfer	steal, dump
transferrer of allegiance	traitor, turncoat, betrayer
transient	vagrant, bum
transnational	multinational
transshipment	smuggling
travel	drift

Favorable	**Critical**
trial and error	successive blunders, repeated bunglings
trip	junket
trusted advisers	cronies, inner clique
unannounced offensive	sneak attack, ambush
uncover	dredge up
undercover	sneaky
undocumented immigrant	illegal alien, wetback
unemployed, the	shiftless, bums, misfits
unerring	deadly
unexpectedly	out of left field
unfortunate	incompetent, ill-conceived
unilateral	arbitrary, capricious
uninhibited	irresponsible, wild
unique	strange, odd, irregular, offbeat, bizarre
United States	President's name followed by Administration
unlucky	incompetent
unpaid labor	slavery

Favorable	Critical
unpredictable	unstable, speculative, insecure
unresolved	disorganized, chaotic, confused
unsteady	clumsy
unsuccessful	futile, bungled
untidy	sloppy, motley, ragtag, scruffy, disorganized, ratty, dirty, filthy, slovenly, careless, messy, chaotic, confused
unusual	weird, strange, bizarre, off the wall, twisted, perverse, queer, warped
unwanted material	garbage, trash, rubbish
uplifting	pious
uprising	rebellion, mutiny, insurrection
urgent	last-minute
use	exploit, take advantage of, play with

Favorable	Critical
vacation	junket
variable	erratic, capricious, bizarre, hodgepodge
varied	hodgepodge, messy, jumbled, in disarray, a collection, disparate, erratic, irregular, contradictory
varied experience, one with	journeyman
variegated	jumbled
varying judgments	erraticism, confusion
venerable	outdated, old, ancient, worn out, rickety
veteran	over the hill, old, ancient, decadent, obsolete, outdated, elderly, has-been, washed up, worn out, old-line, old-fashioned, creaking
vigorous	arrogant, aggressive
vigorous criticism	ugly criticism
vigorously	running roughshod over, trampling
vision	lucky guess, blind guess, stab in the dark, jaundiced view, stumbling into

Favorable	Critical
visionary	dreamer
voice	propagandist, apologist, mouthpiece, lobbyist
volunteers	mercenaries, hirelings, hired hands, hired guns
vote for	sell (one's) vote to
wait patiently	loiter, languish, waste time, cool one's heels
warn	threaten
warrior	butcher, killer, murderer
wary	scared, frightened, fearful, paranoiac
we	they
welfare recipient	freeloader
well-known	notorious, infamous
were introduced in	hit
whisper	mumble, mutter
white	lily-white
White House, the	Bush's White House
white paper	tract, sheet
widely known	notorious, infamous

Favorable	Critical
widened horizon	excessiveness
wig	rug
wisdom	cliché, old saw
wise	cunning, clever, shrewd
withdraw	turn tail, be routed, run, flee, panic, run in panic, run out, quit
withdraw in haste	turn tail, be routed, run, flee, panic, run in panic, run out, quit
withdraw support from	abandon
withhold	deprive of, deny, exclude
withhold from view	hide
withhold the truth	lie
words alone	words with quotes
workmanlike	tedious, boring
workout specialist	goon
world public opinion	selected editorials from foreign newspapers
write hastily	scribble, scrawl

Favorable	Critical
yearn for	slaver after
young	incompetent, inexperienced
zealous	extremist, fanatic, crank, wild, mad dog

Part Two

Critical-Favorable

Critical	Favorable
abandon	withdraw support from, leave
abrupt	efficient
absurd	incorrect, mistaken
accident	good fortune, good judgment, event
accidental	spontaneous, opportunistic, impromptu
accuse	maintain, report, speak about, speak out about
acne-scarred	rugged-featured
act	presentation, performance, thing
affair	relationship, living together, sharing quarters
affected	sophisticated
afraid	alarmed
aggressive	assertive, vigorous, bold, forceful, self-confident, forthright
agitate	remind, bring to one's attention, ask for, request, petition, prod, espouse
agitator	protester, demonstration leader, assertive spokesperson

Critical	**Favorable**
aimless	irregular
alarm	alert, nudge, forewarn
alibi	reason
allege	assert, declare, proclaim, report, state, speak about, speak out about, reveal, show
aloof	dignified, formal, by the book, correct, reserved
amateur	has potential
ambition	dedication
ambush	surprise offensive, unannounced offensive
anarchy	freedom, liberty
ancient	veteran, senior, experienced, patriarchal, matriarchal, seasoned, time-tested, time-honored, venerable
animal	human being, person
annihilate	execute, kill, dispatch with, reduce the population of, implement a death sentence of
annoy	prod
apologist	advocate, spokesperson, voice, champion of, backer

Critical	Favorable
appease	comfort
appeasement	accommodation, strategic retreat, tactical retreat, strategic withdrawal, tactical withdrawal
appeaser	flexible negotiator
arbitrary	discretionary, at one's choice, unilateral, decisive, tough, strong, assertive
argue	debate
argument	frank exchange of ideas, frank discussion
arm-twist	influence, pressure
arrogant	assertive, vigorous, bold, forceful, proud, confident, self-confident
artificial	own variety of, man-made
assassinate	execute, kill, dispatch with, reduce the population of, implement a death sentence of
attendee	student
avarice	appetite

Critical	Favorable
backdoor	informal, casual
backing down	compromise, strategic retreat, tactical retreat, strategic withdrawal, tactical withdrawal
back-slapper	extrovert, outgoing person
backward	developing, emerging
badger	remind, bring to one's attention
bait	remind, bring to one's attention
banish	expel
bastard	born out of wedlock, love child
beat	strike with emphasis, chastise, discipline
be bothered with	attend to
be deprived of	pay, contribute
beefy	stout, portly, burly, obese, full-figured, heavy-set
belligerent	debate-minded
bellow	raise one's voice, lift one's voice

Critical	Favorable
be routed	fall back, fall back in good order, withdraw, retreat in an orderly way, advance to the rear, withdraw in haste
besmirch	expose
besotted	inebriated
betray	change allegiance, shift allegiance, transfer allegiance
biased	inclined toward, favoring, advocate of
bicker	debate
billingsgate	forceful language
bitch	lady
bizarre	unique, special, one of a kind, offbeat, unusual, different, alternate, eccentric, variable, irregular
black racism	negritude
blame (v.)	charge (v.)
blatant	noted, outstanding, obvious, striking
blimpy	stout, portly, burly, obese, full-figured, heavy-set
blind guess	vision, prediction, inspiration

Critical	**Favorable**
bloated	stout, full, portly, burly, obese, full-figured, heavy-set, large, expansive, enlarged, satisfied, full, satiated, substantial, generous, expanded, increased
bloodthirsty	eager for combat, eager to engage the enemy
blunder into	happen upon
blunt	forthright, frank
boast	point with pride
bomber	explosives expert, explosives technician
bombing	air support
boneheaded	not quite accurate, erroneous, mistaken, off-target, off-the-mark, imprecise, in error, retarded
boor	rustic person
boorish	unsophisticated
boot out	terminate, exclude, oust, discharge
boring	restful, peaceful, quiet, tranquil, routine, standardized, stable, secure, workmanlike, serious, regular

Critical	Favorable
boss (n.)	dominant leader
boss (v.)	direct, lead, manage
bother (v.)	investigate, probe, examine
brash	bold
brag	point with pride
branded	called, termed
brainwash	educate
brainwashing	news, information, evidence, fact
brash	self-confident, assertive
brawn	muscle
brazen	noted
breed (n.)	group (n.)
bribe	informal contribution
brooding	introspective
brothel	sexual convenience center
brutal	forceful, decisive, strong, determined, assertive, tough, stern
bulky	stout, portly, burly, obese, full-figured, heavy-set
bullet	restraint projectile

Critical	Favorable
bully	remind, bring to one's attention
bullying	decisive, tough, strong, assertive
bum	down on his luck, unemployed, beachcomber, transient, temporary resident
bungled	unsuccessful
Bush	President Bush, the President
Bush Administration, the	the Administration
Bush's White House	the White House
business as usual	adherence to tradition
but	and
butcher (n.)	warrior, soldier
butcher (v.)	execute, kill, dispatch with, reduce the population of, implement a death sentence of
butt in	interpose
buttress	assist, support, aid, help, subsidize
buy (an argument)	accept (an agreement)

Critical	Favorable
cabal	association, group, alliance, consortium, league, confederation
cagey	bright, intelligent, smart, nimble
called	named
can	terminate, exclude, oust, discharge
caprice	individual choice
capricious	variable, irregular, alternating, unilateral
capture	liberate
careless	informal, casual, irregular, untidy
cartel	association, group, alliance, consortium, league, confederation
casual	easygoing, informal, leisurely, pacing oneself
catastrophe	incident
catchphrase	time-tested expression, popular expression
cavalier	easygoing, informal, leisurely, pacing oneself
censure	criticism

Critical	**Favorable**
chaotic	in flux, in transition, unresolved, untidy, informally aligned, informally arranged
charge	assert, say, state, maintain
chase	advance on, move on, follow, pursue, seek
cheap	inexpensive, budget, discounted, thrifty, frugal
childish	straightforward, direct
churn out	manufacture
circus	ceremony
claim	assert, declare, proclaim, report, state, speak about, speak out about, observe, document
clandestine	confidential, privileged
clever	wise, intelligent, perceptive, sound, prescient, perspicacious, foresighted, bright, smart, nimble
cliché	time-tested expression, popular expression, adage, wisdom

Critical	Favorable
clique	association, group, alliance, consortium, league, confederation, organization, community group, community organization
clout (v.)	strike
clumsy	off-balance, unsteady
cluttered	delightfully cramped
cockiness	enormous self-esteem
cocky	confident, poised, assertive
coddle	cater to
coerce	persuade, convince, influence, convert
coincidence	coordination
cold	dignified, formal, stately, by the book, correct
coldhearted	pragmatic, flexible, practical, hardheaded, fence-sitting
collaborate with	cooperate with, help, aid, assist
collaborator	colleague
collection, a	varied, disparate, heterogeneous, mixed, diverse, miscellaneous, has many contributing elements, eclectic

Critical	Favorable
colonial power	mother country
combative	debate-minded
come to power	assume office, take the reins of government, be elected, be appointed
Commie	socialist, Second World
Communist	socialist, Second World
complain	protest
complaining	cooperative, agreeable
compromising	prudent, careful, perspicacious
con (v.)	persuade, convince, convert
con (n.)	business, enterprise
conceal	secret (v.)
concealed	in reserve, anonymous
conceit	self-esteem
conceited	formal, self-assured, self-possessed
concoct	conceive, formulate, plan, prepare, devise
condescending	gracious, dignified
confused	in flux, in transition, unresolved, untidy, considering alternate options

Critical   ## Favorable

Critical	Favorable
confusing	complex, intricate
confusion	varying judgments
connivance	plan
conquest	annexation
conspiracy	agreement, arrangement, bargain, contract, pact, mutual plan of action
contemptuous	gracious, dignified, stately
contentious	debate-minded
contradictory	diverse, varied
contraption	device, machine, implement, apparatus
control	guide, steer
convoluted	complex
cook up	conceive, formulate, devise
cool one's heels	wait patiently
correct	revise, adjust
counterfeit	own variety of
counterhit	avenge
country bumpkin	rustic person
covered up	confidential, privileged
cowardice	combat fatigue, shell shock, anxiety, neurosis, hysteria

Critical	Favorable
cowardly	prudent, careful, cautious, perspicacious, pragmatic
cower	seek safety
crack	joke, jest
crackpot	inventor
crank	militant, zealous, energetic, dedicated, critical
crank out	produce, manufacture
crave	earnestly desire
crazy	mentally ill, mentally retarded, mentally disturbed
creaking	veteran, senior, experienced, patriarchal, matriarchal, seasoned, time-tested, time-honored
criminal	outside the law
crippled	disabled, afflicted, handicapped
criticize	evaluate, critique
crony	adviser, trusted adviser, friend, associate, colleague
crook	tragic person
crowd	group, organization, community group, community organization

Critical	Favorable
crude	forthright, frank, straightforward, direct, not fully sophisticated
cruel	forceful
cult	group, organization, community group, community organization
cunning	wise, intelligent, perceptive, sound, prescient, perspicacious, foresighted, bright, smart, nimble
curt	efficient
dandy	gentleman
dangerous	highly effective, powerful, potent
deadly	unerring
dead slow	restful, peaceful, quiet, tranquil
deal	agreement, arrangement, bargain, contract, pact, mutual plan of action
death squad	combat team

Critical	**Favorable**
decadent	veteran, senior, experienced, patriarchal, matriarchal, seasoned, time-tested, time-honored
decimate	reduce the population of
defame	expose
deformed	rugged-featured
degenerate	tragic person
deliberate	coincidental, accidental
delinquent	somewhat overdue, in no hurry
demagogue	charismatic leader, assertive leader, dynamic leader
demand	ask for, request, petition
demean	charge, attack, confront
denigration	criticism
deny	withhold, reserve
depose	remove from office
deprive of	withhold
deride	criticize, comment on, critique
deserter	straggler
desperate	anxious, concerned, apprehensive

Critical	Favorable
despot	assertive leader, charismatic leader, dynamic leader
despotism	firm rule
deviant	diverse
device	strategy, plan, approach, method
diatribe	critique, criticism, analysis, forceful language
dictate	direct, lead, manage
dictator	assertive leader
dictatorship	central authority, firm rule
different	special
dilapidated	needing repair
dilettante	aesthete
dirty	informal, casual, irregular, untidy
disadvantaged	different
disaster	incident, occurrence
disdain	avoid
disdainful	proud
disfigured	singularly featured, irregularly featured
disgrace	tragedy

Critical	Favorable
disguised	concealed
disgusting	earthy, candid, frank
dishonest	concealed
disorganized	informal, casual, irregular, untidy, in flux, in transition, unresolved
disparate	varied, diverse
dissident	demonstrator
dissipated	satisfied, full, satiated
disturbance	protest demonstration
divorcée	displaced homemaker
do an about-face	reverse one's position
docile	cooperative, agreeable
doctrines	principles, beliefs
dog and pony show	campaign, performance
dogma	principles, beliefs
dominate	lead
dotty	aged and infirm
doubletalk	creative ambiguity
dragoon	persuade, convince
dreamer	philosopher, visionary
dream up	conceive, formulate

Critical	Favorable
dreary	restful, peaceful, quiet, tranquil, stable, secure, routine, standardized, serious
dredge up	uncover, expose
drift	travel, move on
drunk (adj.)	inebriated
drunk (n.)	alcoholic
dubious	theoretical
dumb	not quite accurate, erroneous, mistaken, off-target, imprecise, in error, retarded, off the mark
dump (v.)	export, put, deposit, ship, transfer, place, put down, place down, lay, lay down
dump (n.)	place
easier	more convenient
eat the dust of	follow
editorializing	journalism
egg on	inspire, encourage
ego	self-esteem, pride
egomania	enormous self-esteem

Critical	Favorable
egotistical	strong-willed, proud, confident
elderly	veteran, senior, experienced, patriarchal, matriarchal, seasoned, time-tested, time-honored
encroach on	enter
enemy	opponent
enforcer	regulator, implementer
engineer (v.)	secure, plan, accomplish, achieve
engorged	satisfied, full, satiated
enlistee	volunteer
enormous	full, large, expansive, enlarged
erratic	variable, irregular, alternating, flexible, varying
error	judgment
excessive	generous
excessiveness	widened horizon
exclude	withhold
excuse (n.)	reason, explanation
expedient	convenient, necessary
exploit	use

Critical	Favorable
exploited	ineffective
exploiter	businessman, capitalist, industrialist, merchant, manufacturer, entrepreneur
explosion	energetic disassembly
extra charge	adjustment
extremist	militant, zealous, energetic, dedicated, critical
fabricate	bend the truth
failure	incomplete success
fairy tale	revered belief
fake	own variety of
fall	liberation
famine	diet
fanatic	militant, zealous, energetic, dedicated, critical, hardworking
fancy (v.)	prefer
fantasy	imagination, creativity
fat	stout, portly, burly, obese, full-figured, heavy-set
fealty	loyalty

Critical	Favorable
fearful	prudent, careful, perspicacious, pragmatic, cautious, wary, circumspect
feisty	assertive
filthy sheet	newspaper, journal, bulletin
female	lady
fiddle with	adjust
fill the coffers	help financially
filthy	informal, casual, irregular, untidy, sexually explicit, sexually frank
finagle	achieve, accomplish
fire (n.)	rapid oxidation
fire (v.)	terminate, exclude, oust, discharge, lay off, discontinue
first name only	title followed by last name, title followed by first name
fix	revise, adjust
fixed income	stable income
flabby	stout, portly, burly, obese, full-figured, heavy-set
flail	chastise
flail back	retaliate
flashy	glamorous, glittering

Critical	Favorable
flaunt	express, display
flee	fall back, fall back in good order, withdraw, retreat in an orderly way, advance to the rear, withdraw in haste
flighty	creative
flimsy	delicate
flophouse	shelter
flunky	subordinate, supporter
follow the lead of	follow
foolhardy	dashing, sweeping, heroic, courageous
fop	aesthete
force (v.)	mandate, direct, require, persuade, convince
forced busing	busing
frantic	anxious, concerned, apprehensive, courageous
freeloader	welfare recipient
frenzied	aroused
frightened	alarmed, curious, wary
frigid	dignified, formal, by the book, correct, stately
frivolous	casual, light, airy

Critical	Favorable
front	covering organization
frosty	dignified, formal, by the book, correct, stately
fulminate against	complain about
funnel money to	help financially
fussy	thorough, cautious, circumspect, careful, precise, fastidious
futile	unsuccessful
gadget	implement
gambit	strategy, plan, approach, method
gamble	possibility, chance, outside chance
gang	association, group, alliance, consortium, league, confederation, organization, community group, community organization, people
gang up	bring group pressure
garbage	surplus, excess, unwanted material
gaudy	glamorous, glittering
get around to	address, handle

Critical	Favorable
get even	retaliate
get even for	avenge
get out of	leave
ghetto	separate neighborhood
gibberish	specialized language, precise expressions, creative ambiguity
gigantic	full, large, expansive, enlarged
gimmick	strategy
give in to	accept (an argument)
give up	surrender, capitulate
giving in	accommodation, compromise, strategic retreat, tactical retreat, strategic withdrawal, tactical withdrawal
gloat	point with pride
glop	portion
glut	excess
glutted	satiated
go belly up	surrender, capitulate
goon	workout specialist
goon squad	enforcement detachment

Critical	Favorable
gossip	indication, clue, report
got the idea of	thought to help by
grab	seize
graffiti painter	artist
grandiose	noted, outstanding
greed	appetite
greedy	thrifty, frugal
grind out	produce, manufacture
gripe	complain
gross	alternate, offbeat, eccentric, indiscreet
guess	estimate, judgment, considered judgment, appraisal, theory, determination
gullible	sincere, honest, enthusiastic
gunner	small-arms expert, small-arms technician
gun-shy	prudent, careful, cautious
gutter politics	street politics
guy	gentleman

Critical	Favorable
hackkneyed expression	adage
hail fellow well met	extrovert, outgoing person
handful	small group
handmaiden	supporter
haphazard	informal
harangue	exhort, encourage, actively support, demonstrate, rally
harass	remind, bring to one's attention, investigate
hard-liner	firm advocate
has-been	veteran, senior, experienced, patriarchal, matriarchal, seasoned, time-tested, time-honored
hasty	quick, swift, emergency
hatchet job	critical examination
hatchet man	implementer, protagonist
haughtiness	avoidance
haughty	gracious, dignified, proud, formal, by the book, correct
have a chip on one's shoulder	protest

Critical	Favorable
hawk (v.)	present, explain, appeal, convince, expound, set forth, persuade, inform, educate
hayseed	rustic person
head count	number of people
heap	arrange
hearsay	news, information, evidence, fact, report
heavy-handed	strong, forceful
hector	remind, bring to one's attention
hedge	qualify, modify
henchmen	employees, friends
hick	rustic person
hidden	anonymous
hide	withhold from view, conceal, secret, keep in reserve, keep from view, retain
hidebound	traditional
hideout	headquarters, home base, home grounds
hinder	delay
hippie	alternate, offbeat, eccentric
hired guns	volunteers, employees

Critical	Favorable
hired hands	volunteers, employees
hirelings	volunteers, employees
hit (v.)	bop
hit (v.)	arrived in, were introduced in
hit man	implementer
hocus-pocus	ceremony, proceeding, ritual, rite, analysis
hodgepodge	varied, disparate, heterogeneous, mixed, diverse, miscellaneous, has many contributing elements, eclectic, irregular, alternating
holed up	secluded, isolated
horde	group, crowd
horny	sexually active
house	home
huckster	salesperson, merchant
huge	substantial, generous, expansive, enlarged, increased, full
humdrum	regular
hunch	considered judgment, determination

Critical	Favorable
hunger	diet
hurried	quick, swift, emergency
hustle	present, explain, appeal, convince, expound, set forth, persuade, inform, educate
hype (n.)	message, commercial, ad, promotion
hype (v.)	present, explain, appeal, convince, expound, set forth, persuade, inform, educate, brief
hyper	alert (adj.), effervescent
hysterical	aroused, frantic
idiotic	not quite accurate, erroneous, mistaken, off-target, off-the-mark, imprecise, mistaken, in error, retarded
ignore	pass up
ill-conceived	unfortunate
illegal	outside the law, necessary
illegal alien	undocumented immigrant
illegitimate	born out of wedlock, love child

Critical	Favorable
imbecilic	not quite accurate, erroneous, mistaken, off-target, off-the-mark, imprecise, mistaken, in error, retarded
immoral	necessary
impeach	remove from office
imperialist	businessman, capitalist, industrialist, merchant, manufacturer, entrepreneur
impetuous	enthusiastic, quick, courageous, heroic
impotent	ineffective
impractical	principled, moral
imprisonment	protective custody, preventive detention
impulse	individual choice
impulsive	dashing
in bad taste	candid, frank
incite	exhort, encourage, actively support
incompetent	unlucky, unfortunate, star-crossed, snake-bitten, learning, apprentice, young
indecisive	considering alternate opinions, fence-sitting

Critical	Favorable
indifferent	easygoing, informal, leisurely, pacing oneself, relaxed, fence-sitting
in disarray	varied, disparate, heterogeneous, mixed, diverse, miscellaneous, has many contributing elements, eclectic
indoctrination	news, information, evidence, fact
indulge	cater to
indulgent	compassionate
inexperienced	learning, apprentice, young, has potential
infamous	controversial, famous, noted, distinguished, well-known
inferior	subordinate, inexpensive
infested with	characterized by, distinguished by
infiltrate	take up residence in, advance on
infiltrator	intelligence agent, intelligence operative
inflated	substantial, generous, expanded, increased

Critical	Favorable
inflexible	adamant, holding firm, sticking by one's guns, principled, prickly, systematic, solid, rock-ribbed, resolute, by the book
in hiding	anonymous
inner clique	trusted advisers
insane	mentally ill, mentally retarded, mentally disturbed
insecure	dynamic, exciting, effervescent, unpredictable
insensitive	pragmatic, flexible, practical, hardheaded, forthright, frank, fence-sitting
insubordinate	maverick, defiant, independent
insular	independent, self-employed, freelance, in private practice
insurrection	revolution, uprising, destiny, manifest destiny, destiny of a people
intemperate	aroused, strongly worded
intentional	accidental
interference	involvement
interrupt	interpose

Critical	Favorable
intimidate	pressure, persuade, convince, remind, bring to one's attention
intractable	determined, insistent
intrude into	enter, interpose
invade	liberate, take up residence in, advance on, move into, take up positions in
invaders	liberators
invasion	manifest destiny, destiny of a people, *Lebensraum*
irregular	unique, special, one of a kind, flexible, varying
irresponsible	uninhibited
isolated	independent, self-employed, freelance, in private practice
jaded	satisfied, full, satiated
jar	alert, nudge
jargon	specialized language, precise expressions
jaundiced view	vision, prediction, inspiration
jeremiad	protest, complaint
joint	place (n.)

Critical	Favorable
journeyman	one with varied experience, one with diversified experience, independent contractor
jumbled	varied, disparate, heterogeneous, mixed, diverse, miscellaneous, has many contributing elements, eclectic, variegated, polyglot, complex, intricate
junior senator	senator
junk	miscellaneous items
junket	trip, vacation, mission, journey
kept secret	in reserve
kickback (n.)	returned funds (n.)
kick out	terminate, exclude, oust, discharge, expel
kidnap	remove, take
killer	warrior, soldier
knuckleheaded	not quite accurate, erroneous, mistaken, off-target, off-the-mark, imprecise

Critical	Favorable
labeled	called, termed
lackeys	subordinates, supporters, forces
lacking in principle	prudent, careful, perspicacious, pragmatic
lag	move deliberately, move slowly
lair	headquarters, home base, home grounds
languish	wait patiently
lardlike	stout, portly, burly, obese, full-figured, heavy-set
lash out	struggle (v.)
last-minute	urgent
last name only	title followed by last name
late	somewhat overdue, in no hurry
lax	compassionate
lazy	easygoing, informal, leisurely, pacing oneself
less than	more than (a lesser amount)
lesser	subordinate
lethal	potent, overwhelming, overpowering

Critical	Favorable
lethargic	peaceful
libel (n.)	news, information, evidence, fact
libel (v.)	charge, attack, confront
license	freedom, liberty
lie (n.)	evasion
lie (v.)	bend the truth, withhold the truth
lily-white	all-white, white, Caucasian
lined	rugged
lobbyist	advocate, spokesperson, voice, champion of, backer
lofty	principled, moral
loitering	standing temporarily, waiting patiently
lone	independent, self-employed, freelance, in private practice
loony	mentally ill, mentally retarded, mentally disturbed
loot	revenue, money, reparations
lose control	slacken one's hand
loser	down on his luck
lost to	gained by (another party)

Critical	Favorable
lot	group, people, community
loud	outspoken
loudmouth	protester, demonstrator, assertive spokesperson
lower	subordinate
luck	good fortune, good judgment
lucky	accurate, correct, skilled, fortunate
lucky guess	vision, prediction, inspiration, good judgment
lumber	move heavily
lump together	consolidate
lunatic	mentally ill, mentally retarded, mentally disturbed
lust for	earnestly desire
lying	phrase laundering
machine	efficient political organization, smooth-running political organization
macho	proud
mad	mentally ill, mentally retarded, mentally disturbed

Critical	Favorable
mad dog	militant, zealous, energetic, dedicated, critical
make	require
make up	formulate, prepare
male	gentleman
malnutrition	diet
malpractice	judgment
man	gentleman
maneuver	strategy, plan, approach, method
manipulable	cooperative, agreeable
manipulate	plan
masochistic	self-sacrificing, altruistic
massacre (v.)	kill
massive	substantial, large
maudlin	poignant, moving
mawkish	poignant, moving
meddling	involvement
meek	cooperative, agreeable
mercenaries	volunteers, employees

Critical	**Favorable**
messy	varied, disparate, heterogeneous, mixed, diverse, miscellaneous, has many contributing elements, eclectic, informal, casual, irregular, untidy, polyglot, variegated
mincing	delicate, prim, careful
minions	forces
miserly	financially cautious, parsimonious, financially conservative, careful with money, frugal
misfits	the unemployed
mishap	event
mob	group, organization, community group, community organization, crowd
mob rule	popular democracy
mob scene	protest demonstration
mock	criticize, comment on, critique
mole	intelligence agent, intelligence operative
mollify	reassure, comfort
mongrel	ethnically diverse

Critical	Favorable
monopoly	exclusive
monstrous	substantial, generous, expansive, increased
moody	introspective
morbid	grim
moronic	not quite accurate, erroneous, mistaken, off-target, off-the-mark, imprecise, mistaken, in error, retarded
motley	informal, casual, irregular, untidy
mouth	assert, declare, proclaim, report, state, speak about, speak out about
mouthpiece	advocate, spokesperson, voice, champion of, backer, lawyer, attorney
muckraking	journalism
mugger	young man
multinational	transnational
mumble	speak softly, whisper
murder (v.)	execute, kill, dispatch with, reduce the population of, implement a death sentence of, alter the health of, terminate, put to death

Critical	Favorable
murderer	warrior, soldier
muscle (n.)	enforcement detachment
muscle (v.)	persuade, convince
mutinous	defiant
mutiny	revolution, uprising
mutt	ethnically diverse
mutter	speak softly, whisper
myth	traditional belief, popular belief, popular wisdom, traditional wisdom, revered belief, revered wisdom, folk belief, folk wisdom
nag	remind
naive	straightforward, direct, sincere, honest, simple, clear
name alone	name preceded by title
name or term preceded by "so-called"	name or term alone
narrow	selective
narrow interest	specialization
native (n.)	local inhabitant, resident, indigenous person

Critical	Favorable
ne'er-do-well	beachcomber, transient, temporary resident, down on his luck, unemployed
nervous	alert
neurotic	security-conscious
nit-pick	argue, debate, argue a fine point
nit-picking	thorough, cautious, circumspect, careful, precise, fastidious
noble	principled, moral
noisy	outspoken
nonsense	creative ambiguity
nonsensical	not quite accurate, erroneous, mistaken, off-target, off-the-mark, imprecise
nostrum	solution
notion	plan, program, formula
notorious	controversial, famous, noted, distinguished, well-known, prominent, widely known
nuisance	agitator, harasser
nutty	mentally ill, mentally retarded, mentally disturbed

Critical	Favorable
obscene	earthy, sexually explicit, sexually frank
obsequiousness	loyalty
obsessed with, be	concentrate on, focus on
obsolete	veteran, senior, experienced, patriarchal, matriarchal, seasoned, time-tested, time-honored, conservative, traditional
obstinate	adamant, determined, insistent
obstruct	delay
obvious	clear
occupation	liberation, manifest destiny, destiny of a people, *Lebensraum*
odd	unique, special, one of a kind
offbeat	unique, special, one of a kind
offhand	easygoing, informal, leisurely, pacing oneself
off the wall	offbeat, unusual, different, alternate, eccentric
old	veteran, senior, experienced, patriarchal, matriarchal, seasoned, time-tested, time-honored, venerable, classic

Critical	Favorable
oldest member	dean
old-fashioned	veteran, senior, experienced, patriarchal, matriarchal, seasoned, time-tested, time-honored, venerable, conservative
old hat	tradition
old-line	veteran, senior, experienced, patriarchal, matriarchal, seasoned, time-tested, time-honored, venerable, conservative
old man	patriarch, senior citizen, golden-ager
old practice	tradition
old saw	wisdom
old wives' tales	traditional belief, popular belief, popular wisdom, traditional wisdom, revered belief, revered wisdom, folk belief, folk wisdom
old woman	matriarch, senior citizen, golden-ager
ominous	meaningful
only	over (for amount to be emphasized)

Critical	Favorable
opinion	news, information, evidence, fact, analysis, estimate, judgment
order	mandate, direct, instruct
ostentatious	glamorous, glittering
outdated	veteran, senior, experienced, patriarchal, matriarchal, seasoned, time-tested, time-honored, venerable
outlandish	eccentric
outlaw	maverick
out of control	aroused
out of left field	spontaneously, unexpectedly
out of one's mind	mentally ill, mentally retarded, mentally disturbed
outstretched palms	recipients
overcautious	circumspect
overrun	liberate
oversexed	sexually active
over the hill	veteran, senior, experienced, patriarchal, matriarchal, seasoned, time-tested, time-honored

Critical	Favorable
pal	adviser, supporter, associate, colleague
pander to	cater to
panic (n.)	concern
panic (v.)	fall back, fall back in good order, withdraw, retreat in an orderly way, advance to the rear, withdraw in haste
panicky	anxious, concerned, apprehensive, fearful, alarmed, frantic
paranoiac	cautious, suspicious, wary, careful, prudent, security-conscious
participant	military adviser
pasty-faced	pale
payoff	informal contribution
peculiar	eccentric
peddle	present, explain, appeal, convince, expound, set forth, persuade, inform, educate
peer at	investigate, examine
pennypinching	thrifty, frugal
permissive	easygoing, relaxed, even-tempered

Critical	**Favorable**
persecute	bring to justice, expose
perverse	offbeat, unusual, different, alternate, eccentric
pest	agitator, harasser
pet	selected, preferred
pick up	secure, procure
pick up the pieces	regroup, consolidate
pie in the sky	optimistic projections
pigheaded	adamant
pile	arrange, load, stack
pious	uplifting, earnest, sincere
pipe up	declare, speak out
pitch (v.)	present, explain, appeal, convince, expound, set forth, persuade, inform, educate, brief
platitudes	principles
playground	resort
play with	use
pliant	cooperative, agreeable
plodding	persistent, dogged
plot	strategy, plan, approach, method, program, formula

Critical	Favorable
plug	brief (v.), promote, advertise
politician	statesman, public official, legislator, political figure
pompous	dignified, formal, by the book, correct
pornography	sexual explicitness, sexual realism
pound	strike with emphasis
powerless	ineffective
preach	present, explain, appeal, convince, expound, set forth, persuade, inform, educate, brief, instruct, direct, guide
preacher	clergyman
predatory	aggressive
preferential hiring for minorities	affirmative action
prejudiced	favoring, inclined toward
President's name followed by Administration	United States
pressure (v.)	guide (v.)
pressure group	issue-oriented organization
primal	basic

Critical	Favorable
prissy	thorough, cautious, circumspect, careful, precise, fastidious
privileged	private
profiteer	businessman, capitalist, industrialist, merchant, manufacturer, entrepreneur
promiscuous	sexually active
promise	express intention
promote	present, explain, appeal, convince, expound, set forth, persuade, inform, educate
propaganda	briefing, news, information, evidence, fact, advertising, public opinion, advocacy
propagandist	advocate, spokesperson, voice, champion of, backer
propitious	convenient
prop up	support, subsidize, save, aid, shore up, preserve, assist, help, fortify
proselytize	convert, convince
provocative	strongly worded
prowl	patrol
PR person	spokesperson

Critical	Favorable
psychotic	mentally ill, mentally retarded, mentally disturbed
publicity blitz	news coverage
pudgy	compact, chunky
pull off	accomplish, achieve
punch	strike
punish	damage
puppet	subordinate, supporter
pursue	advance on, move on, follow
push	present, explain, appeal, convince, expound, set forth, persuade, inform, educate, guide, advertise, move
push through	legislate, pass
pushy	assertive
pussyfoot	proceed cautiously
queer	offbeat, unusual, different, alternate, eccentric
quibble	argue, debate, argue a fine point
quit	resign, retire, withdraw

Critical	Favorable
rabble	crowd, group
rabble-rouser	demonstration leader
racism	racial pride
racket	business, enterprise
radical	liberal, progressive, creative
rag	newspaper, journal, bulletin, publication
ragtag	informal, casual, irregular, untidy
rag trade	fashion industry, garment industry
rail against	inveigh against
rake in	collect, make, gather
ram through	move decisively
rant (v.)	assert forcefully
rant (n.)	complaint
rash	indiscreet
rationalization	analysis, explanation
ratty	informal, casual, irregular, untidy
raving	mentally ill, mentally retarded, mentally disturbed
raw	apprentice

Critical	Favorable
reaction	opposition
reactionary	conservative, traditional
rebellion	revolution, uprising, destiny, manifest destiny, destiny of a people
reckless (adj.)	emergency (adj.)
redneck	rustic person
refuse	not accept
retreat	redeploy
regime	government, council, state, administration
regimented	systematic, disciplined
relief	social transfer payments, human services, special services
religionist	clergyman
repeated bunglings	several tries
repetitive	consistent
repulsive	candid, frank
restrict	restrain
retarded	special
reverse racism	affirmative action
rickety	venerable, seasoned, time-tested

Critical	Favorable
riddled with	characterized by
ridicule	comment on
ridiculous	incorrect, mistaken
rigid	solid, rock-ribbed, formal, by the book, correct, consistent
riot (v.)	demonstrate
riot (n.)	protest demonstration
rip-off	bargain
road show	campaign
rogues' gallery	list
rubbish	surplus, excess, unwanted material
rude	efficient, not fully sophisticated
rug	hairpiece, wig
rules	principles, beliefs
rule the roost	be in charge
ruling circles	government, council, state, administration
ruling clique	government, council, state, administration
rumor	news, information, report, evidence, fact, indication, clue

Critical	Favorable
run	fall back, fall back in good order, withdraw, retreat in an orderly way, advance to the rear, withdraw in haste
run across	encounter (v.)
run after	pursue, seek, follow
run around	circulate, socialize
run away	seek safety
run-down	needing repair
run in panic	fall back, fall back in good order, withdraw, retreat in an orderly way, advance to the rear, withdraw in haste
running roughshod over	forcefully, decisively, vigorously
running wild	freedom, liberty
run out	resign, retire, withdraw
same old song	same reason
savage	potent, overwhelming, overpowering, tough, stern, forceful, eager for combat, eager to engage the enemy, determined, no holds barred
scab	independent worker

Critical	Favorable
scalding	critical
scam	business
scandal	sensation
scared	cautious, wary
scarred	rugged-featured
scathing	critical
scheme	strategy, plan, approach, method, program, mutual plan of action, formula, enterprise
scornful	proud, critical
scrape up	gather, collect, garner, deliver
scrawl	write hastily
scream	raise one's voice, lift one's voice, assert forcefully
scribble	write hastily
scruffy	informal, casual, irregular, untidy
secret	confidential, privileged, anonymous
seesawing	alternating
segregated	private
seize power	assume office, take the reins of government, be elected, be appointed

Critical	Favorable
selected editorials from foreign newspapers	world public opinion
self-righteous	correct, earnest
self-serving document	advertisement, promotion
self-styled	independent, self-employed, freelance, in private practice
self-styled writer	journalist
sell	present, explain, appeal, convince, expound, set forth, persuade, inform, educate
sell (one's) vote to	vote for
senator	senior senator
senile	aged and infirm
set in one's ways	traditional, conservative
severe	substantial
sexual deviation	sexual preference
sexual perversion	sexual preference
sexual queerness	sexual preference
shabby	inexpensive, economical
sheet	newspaper, journal, bulletin, publication, position paper, white paper
shiftless	the unemployed

Critical	Favorable
shifty	bright, intelligent, smart, nimble
shoddy	informally prepared, inexpensive, budget, discounted
short	efficient
shot back	responded forcefully
shout	raise one's voice, lift one's voice
shove	move, direct, guide, steer
show	presentation, performance, thing
showy	dashing
shrewd	wise, intelligent, perceptive, sound, prescient, perspicacious, foresighted, bright, smart, nimble
shriek	raise one's voice, lift one's voice
simpleminded	straightforward, direct, simple, clear
sitting duck	lacking adequate defense
sketchy	brief (adj.)
skinny	thin, slight, slender

Critical	Favorable
slander	news, information, evidence, fact, charge, attack, confrontation
slanted	inclined toward, favoring
slaughter	execute, kill, dispatch with, reduce the population of, implement a death sentence of
slaver after	earnestly desire, yearn for
slavery	unpaid labor
slave state	socialist, Second World
slick	bright, intelligent, smart, nimble
slink	move stealthily
slogan	time-tested expression, popular expression, principle
sloppy	informal, casual, irregular, untidy
slothful	easygoing, informal, leisurely, pacing oneself
slovenly	informal, casual, irregular, untidy
slow	restful, peaceful, quiet, tranquil, deliberate, leisurely
slur (v.)	charge, attack, confront, accuse

Critical	Favorable
sly	bright, intelligent, smart, nimble
smear	exposé, attack
smear on	apply
smuggle	keep from view, conceal, retain
smuggling	transshipment
smut	sexual explicitness, sexual realism
sneak	move stealthily, keep from view, conceal, retain
sneak attack	surprise offensive, unannounced offensive
sneaky	covert, hidden, undercover, concealed
sneering	proud
snipe at	investigate
snoop on	investigate, examine
soft	compassionate, easygoing
soft-liner	flexible negotiator
song-and-dance act	presentation, performance, thing
special interests	national security
special privilege	priority

Critical	Favorable
specimen (of a person)	example (of a person)
speculation	possibility, chance, outside chance
speculative	dynamic, exciting, effervescent, unpredictable
spent time	served
spoiling for a fight	eager to engage the enemy
spotty record, a	many successes
spout	proclaim, declare, state, expound, set forth
spy	intelligence agent, intelligence operative
spy on	investigate, examine, monitor, observe, put under surveillance, study
squat	compact, chunky
stab in the dark	estimate, judgment, vision, prediction, inspiration
stagnant	stable
stalk	pursue
startle	alert (v.)
static	consistent
steal	transfer, remove, take

Critical	Favorable
sticks, the	rural environment or areas, rustic environment or areas, bucolic environment or areas
stiff	systematic
stingy	financially cautious, parsimonious, financially conservative, careful with money, frugal
stodgy	stable, secure, serious, reliable
stoopingly	graciously
stop cold	delay, postpone
straddling the fence	middle-of-the-road
straggle	move deliberately, move slowly
strange	offbeat, unusual, different, alternate, eccentric, unique, special, one of a kind
straw man	illustration, example, instance
strident	forceful, assertive
strike	bop
strikebreaker	independent worker
strong-arm (adj.)	decisive, tough, strong, assertive
strong-arm (v.)	persuade, convince

Critical	Favorable
strongman	dominant leader
strongman's crony	official
strip (v.)	require, exact (v.)
stubborn	adamant, holding firm, sticking by one's guns, principled, prickly, persistent, determined, insistent
stuffed shirt	dignified, formal, by the book, correct
stuffy	formal, proper
stumble on	encounter, happen upon
stumbling into	vision, prediction, inspiration
stupid	not quite accurate, erroneous, mistaken, off-target, off-the-mark, imprecise, in error, retarded
successive blunders	trial and error
supercilious	proud
superficial	brief, summary
superstition	traditional belief, popular belief, popular wisdom, traditional wisdom, revered belief, revered wisdom, folk belief, folk wisdom
supply	give

Critical	Favorable
susceptible	honest
suspicious	cautious, careful, security-conscious
suspiciously	possibly, probably
swarm (n.)	group, organization, community group, community organization, crowd
swarm (v.)	gather, congregate, assemble
swarming with	characterized by, distinguished by
swindle	enterprise
swipe	swing
sycophant	subordinate, supporter
tactic	strategy, plan, approach, method, move
take	receipts
take advantage of	use
take directions from	follow
takeover	annexation, absorption, acquisition
talk (one) into	persuade, convince, convert
tawdry	sexually explicit, sexually frank

T

Critical	Favorable
teacher	educator
tear-jerking	poignant, moving
tedious	deliberate, leisurely, workmanlike, routine, standardized
tentacles	outreach
terrorism	manifest destiny, destiny, destiny of a people
terrorist	freedom fighter, guerrilla, irregular warrior, armed revolutionary, liberator
they	we
thief	tragic person
threaten	warn
threatening	forthright, assertive
throw at	present to, contribute to
throw in the towel	surrender, capitulate
throw out	oust, exclude, expel
thump	strike with emphasis
tight	thrifty, frugal
timid	prudent, careful, perspicacious, pragmatic, cautious
tinkerer	inventor

Critical	Favorable
tirade	protest, complaint, forceful language
title preceded by "self-styled"	title only
toady	subordinate, supporter
toadying	cooperative, agreeable
toss	place, put
toss out	propose
totalitarian	authoritarian
tract	publication, position paper, white paper
trail behind	follow
traitor	transferrer of allegiance
trampling	forcefully, decisively, vigorously
transparent	clear
trappings	symbols
trash	surplus, excess, unwanted material
trick	practical joke, strategy
tricky	miraculous
trivial	airy
trot out	introduce, present

Critical	Favorable
truckler	subordinate, supporter
try to sell to	brief (v.)
turncoat	transferrer of allegiance
turn down	not accept
turn tail	fall back, fall back in good order, withdraw, retreat in an orderly way, advance to the rear, withdraw in haste
twisted	offbeat, unusual, different, alternate, eccentric
two cents' worth	contribution
typical	classic
tyrannical	decisive, tough, strong, assertive, authoritarian
tyranny	firm rule, central authority
tyrant	assertive leader, charismatic leader, dynamic leader
ugly	singularly featured, irregularly featured
ugly criticism	vigorous criticism
uncertain	careful, deliberate, moderate
underdeveloped	developing, emerging
underhanded	concealed, covert

Critical	Favorable
undisciplined	creative
unload	deposit
unstable	dynamic, exciting, effervescent, unpredictable
untried	has potential
up to	doing, engaged in
used	previously owned
utterance	statement, declaration
vacillating	alternating
vagrant	transient, temporary resident, beachcomber
vague	imprecise
vain	proud
vengeful	justice-seeking
vicious	tough, stern, forceful, potent, overwhelming, overpowering, decisive, strong, assertive, determined, no holds barred
vindictive	justice-seeking
violence	liberation

Critical	**Favorable**
want	need, require
warmonger	military adviser
warped	alternate, offbeat, eccentric, unusual
washed up	veteran, senior, experienced, patriarchal, matriarchal, seasoned, time-tested, time-honored
waste time	wait patiently
weak	easygoing, relaxed, even-tempered, delicate
weird	offbeat, unusual, different, alternate, eccentric
welfare	social transfer payments, human services, special services
wetback	undocumented immigrant
whim	individual choice, creativity
whine	protest, complain
whip	chastise
whip up	exhort, encourage, actively support
whorehouse	sexual convenience center
wild	militant, zealous, energetic, dedicated, critical, uninhibited

Critical	Favorable
wily	bright, intelligent, smart, nimble
wishy-washy	flexible
with a scowl	in righteous indignation
with a snarl	in righteous indignation
wither	isolate, neutralize
withering	critical
woman	lady
words with quotes	words alone
workaholic	hard worker, dedicated
worn out	veteran, senior, experienced, patriarchal, matriarchal, seasoned, time-tested, time-honored, venerable
wrest from	exact
yell	raise one's voice, lift one's voice
yes-man	subordinate, supporter

An Invitation to You

If you have advocacy words that you would like to send us, we invite you to do so for possible inclusion in a subsequent edition of this book. You should know that no compensation or credit can be given, no submitted materials will be acknowledged or returned, and only appropriate suggestions would be included. But our thanks to you in advance.

About the Author

William Drennan is president and editorial director of Drennan Communications, a literary firm in New Hampshire. In a book publishing career spanning the past forty-seven years, Mr. Drennan, a native New Yorker, has served as editor, copy editor, and agent. He and his wife, Christina, are parents of a daughter, Caroline, and a son, William.